CW00500173

The Wrong Ancient Mariner

(and other variant verses)

by

Martin Parker

Grosvenor House
Publishing Limited

This book is published by
Grosvenor House Publishing Ltd
Link House
140 The Broadway, Tolworth, Surrey, KT6 7HT.
www.grosvenorhousepublishing.co.uk

A CIP record for this book
is available from the British Library

ISBN 978-1-80381-608-1

Martin Parker's light verse has appeared in a variety of national publications including The Spectator, The Literary Review, The Daily Mail and The Oldie as well as online sites including Light (USA) and Lighten Up Online which he founded in 2008.

His 2017 collection, *I Think I Thought*, proved an ideal gift for those who are really difficult to buy presents for – a welcome change from the usual golf balls, pot-plants or socks! So welcome, in fact, that a reprint is now a possibility.

Martin now lives in Dorset where he can be reached either via his website at:–

www.martinparker-verse.co.uk

or by email to:–

martin@martinparker-verse.co.uk

What People Are Saying About This Book

"There's a spelling mistake on Page..."
        (The Times Literacy Supplement.)

"Following a complaint from a customer in Stratford-upon-Avon we have greatly improved our pre-delivery checks procedure."
        (The CEO, Ikea.)

"I have every confidence in Ms Ayres's teeth."
        (Her dentist.)

"Thanks to this book my wife now runs an exceedingly good bakery business."
        (Rudyard Kipling, retired writer.)

"Even more enjoyable than my birthday."
        (Eeyore.)

"Much more entertaining than the prospect of Tennyson's garden."
        (Maud.)

"A far better present than roses and only a fraction less desirable than a limousine."

(Dorothy Parker. (No relation.))

"More enjoyable, even, than tennis."

(Joan Hunter-Dunn.)

"We must stress that a balanced diet requires more than bison products alone."

(The B.M.A.)

"We can assure Mr. Williams that our product is just as healthy as plums and also keeps very well in a fridge."

(The CEO, Pot Noodle Ltd.)

"Please note that I no longer care for Guardsmen, nor did I ever kiss Christopher Robin goodnight."

(Alice.)

"A muse of fire that doth approach the brightest heaven of invention."

(W.S. Stratford-upon-Avon.)

CONTENTS

A Poet's Lot is Not a Happy One:—

Aspects of Love:—

Festive Cheer:—

CONFESSIONS
and
REVELATIONS

The Rime of the Wrong Ancient Mariner

My name is Coleridge, Samuel Taylor.
On the road I met a sailor
Who grasped my hand with iron grip
And told me of his sailing trip
And how, not far from Lowestoft,
He'd met a storm-tossed Albatross.

A story stirred within my head.
I asked, *"What then?"* The sailor said,
"The March winds blew across the sea,
The bird sailed on and so did we.
It was our normal weekly run,
Cold and wet and not much fun,
Dirty, salt-caked, rough and slow
Butting down to Felixstowe
With Tyne coal, pig-lead and cheap tin trays."
(I thought, "That might make a poem one of these days.")

A wild tale grew within my head.
I asked, *"What next?"* The sailor said,
"The bird sailed on and so did we,
It seemed to like our company.
There's nothing more for me to tell
Except our journey ended well." *(Continuing overleaf)*

"This salty son of our proud nation,"
I thought, *"Has no imagination.*
There's nothing there to please a reader.
What a boring little bleeder!"

"Pray tell," I said, *"I need to know,*
Did you take your trusty bow
And aim it at the great bird's head,
Let fly and kill it stony dead?
And did your crew all starve and die
Gaunt of frame and mad?" said I.
"And did your sails hang limp and slack
And did no crewman make it back,
And was your ship, deprived of motion,
Becalmed upon a painted ocean?"

"Not so," the Mariner replied;
"No-one sickened, no-one died.
The waves rolled on across the sea,
The ship sailed on and so did we."
And though I pressed and begged and urged
No fact of interest emerged,
No hint of tales that might endure
If told in lengthy literature,
Nor cause for readers to disburse
Their cash upon such dreary verse.

All morning he did me regale
With his uneventful tale.
I begged him, *"Was there not one ghost,*

Or, better still, a ghoulish host?
No sea-beasts? Hermit? Pilot Boat?
No thrill in your dull life afloat?
Of epic tale no slightest sign?"

I told him plain the bottom line –
That readers would not give a toss
Unless he'd killed the Albatross.

"Know you," he said, *" 'Twould be absurd*
To kill a talismanic bird.
I've told my tale and now you know it;
There's nothing there to thrill a poet."

But, having wasted half the day,
I wrote *this* poem anyway,
And see another in my dreams
Of galleons and of quinquiremes –
With, to avoid financial loss,
A slaughtered friendly Albatross.

Game, Set and Match!

(John Betjeman died in 1985, Joan H-D in 2008)

I was Joan Hunter-Dunn, *your* Joan Hunter-Dunn
whose ardour soon cooled in the Aldershot sun.
For your tennis was poor and your idea of fun
was to sit in the car park till twenty to one
without your attempting the slightest attack
on my baseline defence. So I gave the ring back,
having realised that, married, we'd spend all our time
with you counting stresses and searching for rhyme.
But a suntanned young Aldershot goddess has needs
and mine were not little rhymed verses, but deeds.
So I married another, more dashing, instead,
who was better than you at both tennis and bed.
    And now you're long dead while I'm still having fun.
    So it's game, set and match to Miss Joan Hunter-Dunn.

John Betjeman's
Surprising Saturday Job

(a fantasy written for a *Spectator* competition)

Her fish-netted thighs left me weak at the knees
As I climbed up behind her towards our trapeze;
Then standing surveying the crowd from the heights,
She in her sequins and me in my tights,

And the Aldershot subalterns cheering her charms
As she flew her parabolas into my arms,
And their gasps of alarm as she'd plummet and twist
Till I grasped her and clasped her by ankle and wrist.

And the thrill of her touch and the throb of each nerve
As she'd hang from my legs in a sinuous curve,
And the joy that would come, as I gathered her in,
From the nearness of sequins and tennis-tanned skin.

And the swing-along, cling-along ring-a-ding-dong
Of my old part-time job at The Star-Spangled Thong;
And the furtive and hopelessly guilt-ridden fun
Of those poetry-free nights with Miss Joan
Hunter-Dunn.

Bloody Woman from Dakota

Me the ancient squaw, Nokomis,
Guardian to young Hiawatha.
Hiawatha foolish dreamer,
Him in love with young Dakota
Maiden, name of Minnehaha.
Her name it mean Laughing Water,
Silly name for someone's daughter.

    Him decline the local talent,
    Him get lovesick, … sulky, … acne.
    Him say he want make a treaty
    With the fearsome tribe, Dakota.
    Me say, *"Bring no foreign floosies*
    To the wigwam of Nokomis."

Hiawatha, all love-sickly,
Spurn the love of Old Nokomis,
Pay no heed to guardian's wailing.
Ingrate child, him set off hotly
To the land of the Dakota,
Shoot a red deer, take it, grovelling,
To the wigwam of her father.

    Silly boy, he break my heart. He
    Win the hand of Minnehaha,
    Bloody woman from Dakota,

Bring her home to me, Nokomis.
Now I'm stuck with her for daughter,
Minnehaha, Laughing Water.

Hot on trail comes travelling poet,
Write in lines with maddening metre
Of the tale of Hiawatha.
Me, Nokomis, dead against it,
Knowing White Man speak with fork tongue,
Want our country, covet bison.
Tale soon bring in gawping tourists.

Sensing profit me turn tepee
Into trendy ethnic café,
Serve authentic local specials
For the rubbernecking grockles.
Bison scrag-end, bison entrails.
Serve them right, says Hiawatha.

Minnehaha's Bison Breakfasts

Old Nokomis she served bison
For my breakfast every week-day;
Cold, grey bits of boring bison
Served up in the same old bleak way.

Minnehaha go to college.
She learn many other dishes;
Scrambled bison, bison porridge,
Food surpassing young brave's wishes;

Bison fritters, bison mornay,
Bison with a squirrel purée,
Bison trifle, bison brulée,
Bison fondue, bison sorbet.

Me now marry Minnehaha
For her brilliant breakfast know-how.
Minnehaha she will go far;
Old Nokomis she can go now.

Despite Thy Snoring

(with apologies to Ernest Dowson and his Cynara)

Last night 'twixt Morpheus and me there came
that roar.
Once more from out thy lips thy breath was shed
into the night and rattled every door
as I was kept awake by thy damned roaring.
Yet, though my dreams of passion have long fled.
I have stayed faithful to thee, my dear, despite thy
snoring.

I've longed for sleep's caress throughout each night,
for sleeping partner who might lie more quiet,
for remedies to soothe my hapless plight
as I was kept awake by thy damned roaring.
I've thought of murder, but forborne to try it.
I have stayed faithful to thee, my dear, despite thy
snoring.

No respite have I ever found at night for what is
your lack of good control of inhalation
or malformation of your epiglottis
as I am kept awake by your damned roaring.
God only knows why, in my desperation,
I have stayed faithful to thee, my dear, despite thy
snoring.   *(Continuing overleaf)*

Each thunderous night I seek for sweet relief
by means of bigger earplugs and a sleeping pill.
Yet find I no respite, not even brief,
as I am kept awake by thy damned roaring.
Yet, though it takes increasing strength of will,
I have stayed faithful to thee, my dear, despite thy
snoring.

A Confession from Robert Burns

(author of the celebrated '*Address to a Haggis*')

I must confess wha' seems scarce credible:
I ne'er did find the haggis edible.
Nae dram there was could get me tight
enow tae swallow one wee bite.

But, buttered, bashed, most welcome neep,
'tis thee on whom Scots pipes should heap
wi' skirling notes o' vaunti sound
their praise when Burns Night comes around.

For 'twas the braw neep's sonsie face
that saved this Rabbie the disgrace
of throwing up upon the floor
that dish which stuck sae in his craw.

Fair sonsie unsung neep, your place
is chieftain o' the root-veg race
A toast to thee, this Rabbie's saviour,
for smothering yon haggis flavour.

The Boy Wordsworth's Kitten

(after '*She Dwelt Among The Untrodden Ways*')

We lived beside the River Dove.
I had a little kitten
but found her really hard to love
after I'd been bitten.

A manky ball of tooth and claw
she'd hiss and scratch and bite me,
until the day I grimly swore
she would no longer fright me.

She lived unloved and none did know
how Kitty ceased to be.
But now I'm free of her, and oh,
the difference to me!

There's nothing now of her but smell.
She neither hears nor sees,
rolled round our dark infernal well,
a sodden corpse with fleas.

Inn-keeping in the Pyrenees

(after Hilaire Belloc's *'Tarantella'*)

Do you remember our Inn, Amanda?
Do you remember our Inn?

And the wildly rising tones of the honeymooners' groans
which maintained their raucous peak for a solid
god-damned week
in the room which was just next door to our own?

And the B O from Camilla, our boss-eyed Basque guerilla
who attempted, for a laugh, to blow up guests and staff?
and our chef who only cooked stuff from a tin?

And our problem with the bedding and the rash that it
was spreading,
and how we were abused when guests' credit cards refused
to pay up every time we fed them in?

And that tiresome English poet who, wouldn't you just
know it,
while you and I were skint went and earned himself a mint
by passing off our stories as his own?

I wish I could forget but the memory's with me yet.
And the rash! – against the itch of which I doubt I'll win.

You're Still Old, Father William

You're still old, Father William, the young woman said,
And though you're just back from the gym
I really can't see any difference at all
From your workout and sauna and swim.

"I'm a well toned Adonis," he said with a smile,
"According to Mandy my Trainer.
When I say that I'm off to the shower for a while
It's really quite hard to restrain her.

"In my gym," he continued, "my six-pack's renowned
Among all who have glanced thereupon."
Your six-pack, she said, *almost touches the ground.*
Could it be they're just having you on?

At a glance, said the girl, *I can instantly tell*
That beneath your designer apparel
There's no tempting six-pack but more of a ... well,
More of an overfilled barrel.

You're still old, said the girl, *and, from what I can see,*
The gym's made no difference at all.
You still can't do press-ups, or bend at the knee
Or stand yourself up when you fall.

"In my gym," said the man, "they think I'm a star
And I've recently won a certificate"
Stroll on! said the girl. *It is clear what you are
Is a gullible fool–and in triplicate!*

You sad, vain old man, she said, *listen to me.
Have you flushed all your brains down the dunny?
You are way beyond help. Can you really not see
That all that they want is your money?*

The Dreams of a
Perpetual Twelfth Man

(after Leigh Hunt's '*Abou Ben Adhem*')

I whose batting average stands at nought
Awoke one night from dreams in which I thought
I'd seen God writing out a list of blokes
Accompanied by England's Captain, Stokes.
And to these deities I boldly said,
What do you write? The Almighty raised his head;
The list of those to play in next week's game.
We're almost done. We need just one more name.

As Village Groundsman and team's staunchest fan
Long hoping for promotion from Twelfth Man
I humbly begged them, *Please, I pray,*
Write mine as one who longs, just once, to play.
The Godheads laughed and vanished. Then next night
They came again with broad smiles shining bright
And showed the names picked for the Second Test.
And, lo! My own led all the famous rest.

Morning in a Different Light

(with apologies to both Omar Khayyam
and Edward Fitzgerald)

Awake, and Morning in a different Light
Reveals the Girl with whom I spent Last Night.
Without a Drink she's not a pretty Sight.
I hope we didn't, but I think we might.

Thus, many Times did I in Youth frequent
The Sort of Girls of whom I now repent.
Though not without a Smile do I recall
The Memories of many good Times spent.

But, sadly, Youth must vanish with one's Hair
And Lust cannot forever hold back Care.
The Days of Love that make the Rafters ring
Must vanish as a Mist into thin Air.

And as in this Hotel at Break of Day
I strove to love her, straining where we lay
Entwined, suspended from the Chandelier
She urged me, "Faster, Lover; faster, pray!

"You're old; there's not one Moment more to waste
Nor much of Love that's left for you to taste.
Your Light is dimming and its oft-trimmed Wick
Now nears its last faint Glow. So make you Haste.

(Continuing overleaf)

"Soon of the Power to love you'll be bereft.
No more will you weave Passion's Warp and Weft.
Too soon grey Dawn will put your Stars to Flight,
And Memory will then be All that's left.

"No Chance to make one final glorious Pass,
All Efforts to make Love will end in Farce.
No matter how you try there'll be no Chance
To drain Love's last Dregs from your empty Glass."

CHILDREN'S CORNER

City Whizz Kid

(after A A Milne's '*Happiness*')

I've got
Great Big
inherited
Trust Funds;
I've got
money in
mountainous
stacks.

I've got
Great Big
City-whizz
Bonuses.
Floreat Etona
and
Goldman Sachs!

The Haiku at Pooh Corner

doting father's tales
of son's stuffed menagerie
enchant all ages

childhood's toys outgrown
boy and bear live on to play
poohsticks forever

all anthropomorphs
will pledge lifelong devotion
others may throw up*

*(as Dorothy Parker did while reading this book)

The Lion replies to Christopher Robin

(who'd been showing off his home-made tail)

Yes, I'm a lion and I've got a tail
And so has the elephant and so has the whale
And so has the crocodile and also the quail.
But *your* tail's not like ours.

To you a tail is no damned use.
You're a perfect example of tail abuse.
Besides, it's a clip-on and sure to work loose
In less than a couple of hours.

For us a tail is a vital tool
As well as looking extremely cool.
But *you'll* get hell when you go to school
And show yours off in the showers.

Christopher Robin's
Party Animals

There are bottles and fag ends and litter
    and thistles and owl pellets too:
the house is in need of a clean up
    which Nanny refuses to do.
And Piglet is still feeling fragile
    while Pooh's in a comatose snooze.
So it's me who is stuck with the housework
    after the party at Pooh's.

There's honey all over the sofa
    and *vol au vents* blocking the loo.
But clearing up mess while hung over
    is the last thing they're able to do.
It is somebody's turn, says the rota,
    but a wine stain has covered up whose.
So I am the one in the hot seat
    after the party at Pooh's.

The forest is quiet and deserted.
    Last night was a hell of a do.
Now Eeyore and Tigger are missing
    and there's no sign of Kanga and Roo;
and Wol can't do more than just mumble
    some drunken *To-Wits* and *To-Woos*.

(Continuing overleaf)

So I've no hope, again, of assistance
    after a party at Pooh's . . . .

But over the years the thought struck me
    that, with adulthood long overdue,
it was time that I cleared out my Nursery
    though its memories would cling on like glue.
So the faithful old friends of my childhood
    were sent to museums and zoos.
But though I'm now spared all the housework
    I still miss those parties at Pooh's.

Bagpipe Music at Buckingham Palace

(Louis MacNeice writes AA Milne)

It's no go this trip to Town to visit Buckingham
Palace.
And it's no go being dragged along by my Norland
Nanny, Alice.
For Alice is marrying one of the guard and every
lovesick day
She brings me here to watch her stand and ogle her
fiancé.

Alice says his life is hard though a sergeant darns his
socks.
But I hope his toes turn blue with cold in his wretched
sentry-box,
For it's no go Alice's love life when all I want to do
Is hold her hand on a trolleybus and spend the day at
the Zoo.

James James Morrison Morrison Weatherby George
Dupree
Learned his mother was on the streets when he was
only three.

(Continuing overleaf)

Sir Thomas Tom of Appledore gave squeak-free
Hugh a blip
And Owl's bell got a good long pull when Eeyore got
the snip.

But it's no go asking about such things – or kings – since
her replies
Are either trite banalities or sometimes downright lies.
And it's no go that I view her man with a deeply
seething malice
When all I want is nursery tea and a goodnight kiss
from Alice.

Primary School in the Time of Covid

(after Allan Ahlberg's '*Please, Mrs. Butler*')

Please Mrs Butler
You're coughing quite a lot
And you're really hot and sweaty, Miss.
Is Covid what you've got?

Be guided by the science,
And please don't badger me.
Just keep your distance, wash your hands
And fetch my PPE.

It's hard to understand, Miss,
For kids as young as us
Just what Covid is, Miss,
And why there's such a fuss.

The school needs an example, dear,
Of someone who's unwell.
So hurry to Assembly now
And I'll do Show and Tell.

Sing a Song of Sixpence
with Walter de la Mare

(after '*The Listeners*')

"Is there anybody there," said the Blackbird
with a vengeful look in its eye,
while the smell of its baking colleagues
rose up from the royal game pie.

But nobody answered the Blackbird;
no voice, downstairs or up,
spoke out to admit to the *plat du jour*
on which they would shortly sup.

But the greedy King in his counting-house
and the pie-cook washing her smalls,
plus the Queen with her bread and honey,
had heard the Blackbird's calls.

And they heard the screech of its fury, too,
and the sound of beak on bone
and how the birds began to sing
when the pie-cook's nose was gone.

Nursery Rhymes Updated

(after Anon)

Solomon Grundy
Born on Monday,
Confused on Tuesday,
Worried on Wednesday,
The Tavistock Thursday,
Trans on Friday,
Hospital Saturday,
Sally on Sunday.
    And that was the end
    Of Solomon Grundy.

Old Mother Hubbard
Went to the cupboard
To fetch her poor dog a bone.
But when she got there
The cupboard was bare
Save for tofu and rocket and broccoli,
Plus a hectoring note from the Diet Police
Saying, "Feed your poor animal properly."

The Queen of Hearts
She made some tarts
Each one sugar-free.
The Knave of Hearts

Said to the tarts,
"I hope you're not for me!"

I had a little nut tree
and said that it could bear
both a silver nutmeg
and a golden pear.
The Trade Descriptions Office
prosecuted me
for failing to describe it as
a 'hybrid pear/nut tree.'

Humpty Dumpty sat on a wall,
Humpty Dumpty had a great fall.
The Mayor and the Council got into a twitter
and fined Humpty Dumpty for scattering litter.

Straight From the Horse's Mouth

(after John Betjeman's '*Hunter Trials*')

God knows what came over Diana.
She damn nearly gave me a fit
As she fished down my throat with a spanner
When she thought that I'd swallowed my bit.

She's a talentless, spoiled little owner
Though the Pony Club think she's a pearl.
I'm an obstinate, cussed old loner,
A bad tempered, vengeful old churl.

I was dragged to the Ring without pity.
I was not even asked how I felt.
I was simply supposed to look pretty
And take every fence at full pelt.

"Now here's young Diana on Moonbeam,"
Said a voice on a loud microphone.
"She's the cream of our Pony Club Show Team."
I thought, *"Sod it. I want to go home."*

For I hadn't got over the spanner
And my girth was pulled terribly tight.
"Break a leg," said a girl to Diana.
And I thought to myself, *"She just might."*

(Continuing overleaf)

But I minded my thoroughbred manners
And we won with our clearest round yet.
But I hadn't forgotten the spanner;
So I've eaten her Winner's rosette.

A Very Model of a
Conway Stewart Fountain Pen

(after W.S. Gilbert)

I had a very model of a Conway Stewart fountain pen,
A present given to me on the day I reached the age of ten.
It came with Royal Blue ink in a big bottle which would
splosh a lot
And gave me inky fingers which I used to have to wash
a lot.

Its filling mechanism was a lever made depressible,
A method most effective, though for ten-year-olds quite
messible;
Responsible too often for ink spillage and the dreaded
sound
Of parents getting angry when they found Royal Blue
Ink spreaded round.

One day I found my favourite birthday present had just
disappeared.
Carelessness, ill-luck and theft were reasons which at
first I feared.
But after sixty years I'm now quite sure I was mistaken. It
Now seems entirely likely that my parents had just
taken it.

(Continuing overleaf)

I like to think that somewhere there's a very famous Laureate
Who's writing lighter verses of a standard truly aureate.
And this Grand Old Man Of Literature, although he's now senescent, he
Still has the pen belonging to the ink-stained, pre-pubescent me.

A POET'S LOT
IS NOT A HAPPY ONE

The Poet's Song

(after W.S. Gilbert)

A poet's lot is not a happy one
As he tries to make a living from his verse.
There's no recognition, income, fame or fun
For his chance of publication can't be worse.
Too few publishers will help a living poet
By enabling him to get his new work read.
Though the sods may like his work they seldom show it;
They much prefer their poets to be dead.

It's the 'late' ones who bring in vast sums of money.
You can earn a better living once you're dead.
For the struggling current poet it's not funny
That it's corpses who are earning all the bread.
So to make ends meet what I should now be doing
Is to buy a knife and go and cut my throat.
Then my royalties will surely start accruing
When they posthumously publish what I wrote.

Pam Ayres, Still Worrying About Her Teeth

De profundis, Lord, I beg
Restore each childhood ivory peg
To pearly white and free from cavities,
Unspoilt by sugar's sweet depravities,
Each sleeping nerve as yet undrilled,
Each root canal as yet unfilled.
Mea culpa, Domine,
With dental hygiene gone astray
I stand before your Judgement throne,
My gums eroded to the bone,
Repentant dental dust and ashes
With scarce one tooth which truly gnashes.
But though I plead with caried grin
Please see the penitent within
Whose teeth do not, upon the whole,
Reflect the nature of her soul.

To Mrs. Kipling from Rudyard

If you were not a really hopeless cook,
If Mama had taught you anything at all,
If your food was not repulsive in its look
And put off guests each time they come to call.
If you could read a recipe more clearly
And not mix Fahrenheit with Centigrade,
If you would judge your cooking times more nearly,
Then a great deal fewer errors would be made.

If you could learn a lot from trial and error
And surreptitious slurp and furtive lick,
And not give me the sheer and utter terror
Of trying something new and being sick.
If you could bake a rock bun, not a boulder,
And make mince pies from fruit and not raw meat.
If you could manage 'flambé' not just 'smoulder',
And make a sponge less like a thick foam seat.

If you would file your recipes in folders
And learn to wash your hands before you cook,
Take cream out of the fridge before it moulders,
Swear not to improvise, but use a book.
If you could one day light your family's faces
By discovering a really fool-proof way
Of making light and melting pastry cases
That do not weigh a ton and are not grey.

If you could keep the flour from off the ceiling
And not drop dishes on the kitchen floor,
And remember that cooked food is more appealing
If you've turned on the gas and shut the oven door.
If with practice you could work on your mistakes
And beg Divine assistance from Above,
You might just make exceedingly good cakes
And – with my name – we'd make a mint, my love.

Longfellow and a Paper Shredder

Henry Wadsworth takes much umbrage
At your gift of paper shredder,
At unsubtle implication
That my work is long and boring.
So I passed your gift to maiden,
Brand new bride on Reservation.

Minnehaha she now use it
Slicing veg for Hiawatha.

'Julienne' less hard on molars,
More Designer, much more Cheffy
Than great chunks of uncooked veggies.
She now use it, too, for pasta –
Turn lasagne to spaghetti,
Make her tepee trattoria.

Minnehaha she say thank you.

    Henry Wadsworth (still offended.)

The Happy Prince Brought Down

(Oscar Wilde speaks after his sentencing)

Will nobody give me a fresh green carnation
And pour me a last glass of seltzer and hock
To deaden the sound of smug England's elation
As vengeance is wreaked on me here in the dock?

For I, the High Priest of all greenery-yallery,
Am tried by a jury of philistine fools
And condemned by the sneers of the oafs in the gallery
For not playing love by the Queensberry Rules.

So please raise a glass to my glamorous past
When crowds stood and cheered as they cried out for more,
And wish as you drink that my writing will last
And Bosie's not all they'll remember me for.

*"We, as the Jury, with self-righteous thuggery
Will never forgive those who go in for buggery.
And all England knows, after what's come to pass,
That you are a dick-head and Bosie's an arse."*

The Importance of Being Oscar

(after G K Chesterton)

Before reformers changed the Law, and much to
England's shame,
The road to Hell was paved with love that dared not
speak its name,
Much flaunted by one hot-house bloom, a richly gilded lily,
Who hoped that what he practised could be practised
willy-nilly:
Abhorred by some, adored by some, his future bright
and rosy,
The man who went to Reading Gaol by way of pretty Bosie.

For Man hands cruelty to man, and for a harmless deed
Society's propriety condemned him and decreed
The path to his redemption should be long and
stony-hard,
A dreary path, a weary path around a prison yard,
Consigned to shame, resigned to shame among life's
castaways
Before he went to Paradise by way of Père Lachaise.

Seasick Masefield

(who was, indeed, an acute sufferer)

I must go up on deck again and stick my head over the side
Since me on water is very bad news no matter how calm
the tide.
I've spewed ice-cream on The Serpentine in a decorative
cartouche,
Cornettos from many a gondola and bisque from a bateau
mouche.

I've puked my guts on body boards from Croyde to
Carbis Bay,
I've vomited under Putney Bridge on every Boat Race Day.
I've chundered almost instantly on the Broads in a Norfolk
wherry,
While there's precious little I've not chucked up on the
Dartmouth/Kingswear ferry.

And the Second Mate has just walked past with a greasy
bacon butty.
So my innards are now a churning gloop and my face the
shade of putty.
Now all I need is a lessening wind and to find a
sheltered place
Where a man can lose his breakfast and it won't blow
back in his face.

Breakfast with John Masefield

(after his *'Cargoes'*)

Stately English Bentley bearing me and Masefield
towards a regal breakfast in Royal Tunbridge Wells;
with stiffly starched napery,
silver-plated cutlery,
chafing dishes, flunkeys and no kitchen smells.

Gastric juices tingling at the prospect of the banquet
we expect the Royal Borough to serve up for us both;
kedgeree from India,
coffee from Colombia,
croissants, devilled kidneys and smokies from
Arbroath.

But all that we could find was a dirty British café
with a menu far removed from the menu of our dreams
where we breakfasted on fried eggs,
greasy slices, tinned tomatoes,
hash browns, fatty bacon and cold baked beans.

This is Just to Say . . .

(from a disappointed William Carlos Williams)

If you had left
plums
in your fridge

I might
have written
you
a poem.

But half
a Pot Noodle
does not deserve
literature.

Bob Dylan Looks Back

Some thought me a Prophet. They said they believed
that the Secret of Life was a gift I'd received.
So they drank in my words, but they all were deceived
for the world never started a-changing.

And all my disciples achieved was grow old,
for the starving still starve and the cold are still cold
and our Leaders still known for the lies they have told
and there's no sign of anything changing.

For men still make war and we can't understand
how the wild-eyed and wicked can travel the land
with hate in their heart and a gun in their hand
as the world carries on still unchanging.

So what must I do now as chaos descends?
Once the music has died and the poetry ends
must I spend my eternity making amends
for promising times were a-changing?

That's Life!

(on the fiftieth anniversary of the death of Ogden Nash)

From spermery to wormery
via germery and Infirmary.

Once you're conceived
the gloom is unrelieved.

ASPECTS OF LOVE

A Nursery Memory of Mfanwy

(the young John Betjeman's
"*ringleader, tom-boy, and chum to the weak*")

Smiling Mfanwy, beguiling Mfanwy
Changing the bulb in my high-hanging light,
Nanny and mum to me, d-i-y chum to me,
All of my life I have cherished the sight
Of you standing tiptoe there, high on my nursery chair,
Wobbling and laughing and stretching up while
Your skirt rises up to show glimpses of what's below –
Ankles in stockings of flesh-coloured lisle.

Reaching aloft up there, bulb fitted in with care,
Sleeves falling back on your arms bare and bold;
Bright in their new-won light, there to this boy's delight
Suntan's warm glow and their down of soft gold.
Neatest Mfanwy, my sweetest Mfanwy,
Wobbling and flushed as my Teddy and I
Hold both your ankles tight. Old age will never blight
That picture of you and our shared d-i-y.

Joan Hunter-Dunn's Bequest
to John Betjeman

I was a fact, but your poem was fiction,
a totally false though beguiling depiction
of a love you admitted was just wishful thought
by an amorous poet with no flair for sport.
It was fantasy then, although mildly erotic,
and it's fantasy still now we're old and sclerotic.
Though your skill as a poet meant each of us finds
that what never took place still lives on in our minds.

So these are the items I hereby bequeath
to my fantasist poet with stained tombstone teeth –
Two down-at-heel plimsolls, a frayed tennis dress,
my Slazenger racquet with old wooden press
and its shiny worn handle which smells even yet
of mown grass, warm leather, Palmolive and sweat.

Seeing More of 'Celia'

(Perhaps High Holborn was not the only part
of London in which poet Adrian Mitchell
would imagine Celia naked)

… and when I'm tired and miserable
in Bow or Clerkenwell
or Kentish Town or Kilburn
you're naked there as well.

Dejected on the District Line
on many days I've seen
you pink and firm and beddable
at Kew and Parson's Green.

In fact, when truly wretched
and at my most depressed,
there is no part of London
in which you're not undressed.

And every hour of every night
while in my lonely bed
I dream my lips are walking
your naked A to Z.

There Once Was An Heiress . . .

(after AA Milne's '*The Old Sailor*')

There once was an heiress a City Spiv knew
who had so many assets he wanted to screw
that whenever he thought it was time to begin
he couldn't because of the state he was in.

For he quivered with joy at her range of Blue Chips,
and the same at her eyes and her legs and her lips
plus her dark, Page Three eyes and each little pink
tootsie,
and the fact that she'd not even heard of the Footsie.

She fell hook and line for his slick City charms.
She surrendered her Blue Chips, Debentures and arms:
which gave him full range for his City Spiv urgings
to profit from servicing Stock Market virgins.

But one day, confused, in a lather of lust
he savaged her Isas and traded her bust
which made so much money he shamelessly dipped
his snout in her trough till her assets were stripped.

And I think it disgraceful the way he'd behaved.
He'd been cruelly dishonest and wholly depraved.

Dorothy Parker on
a Gift from Robert Burns

(at last! A car instead of yet another perfect rose)

My love has sent a limousine!
It has me in a swoon.
Its engine's like a melodie
That's sweetly played in tune.

So kind is he, this bonnie lad,
So deep in love am I
That I will love him till the day
Its petrol tank runs dry:

Until its petrol tank runs dry
And its wheels refuse to spin.
And then I'll blame the cheapskate sod
Who put too little in.

Then fare thee well, my skinflint love,
And fare thee well for good.
I'll not return your bloody car –
And wouldn't if I could!

Windsor Wedding

(with acknowledgement to John Betjeman's
'*In a Bath Teashop*')

Let's cross our fingers for the love they bear each other
Which has no time, we hope, for race or rank.
He, such an eager Tigger of a Prince,
She, such a smiling, savvy Yank:
Both, at this moment, little lower than the angels
As they start to walk the fickle public's plank.

Loveliest of Buns,
Your Eccles Cake

(after A.E. Housman)

Loveliest of buns, your Eccles Cake
lies warm before me as I take
a nibble at its sugared rim
and glimpse the soft, sweet joys within.

Now, of the many that I've tried
some were cold and pinched and dried.
But your one I can tell, in short,
is worth a dozen of its sort.

And since I've little time to waste
and cannot now resist its taste
I'll gently work my tongue inside
to where its warm, moist secrets hide.

A Love Letter to Wendy Cope

(on first reading her '*Making Cocoa for Kingsley Amis*')

Drive dreams of Amis from your head.
Make real cocoa for me instead.

Louis MacNeice Plays
Bagpipe Music at
Larkin's *Whitsun Weddings*

It's no go the train ride for this flush of Whitsun
weddings,
And it's no go this rush to town for their blushing,
fumbled beddings.
It's no go the drink consumed and the organ's last
crescendo
And the mothers' hats and the uncle's speech packed
full of innuendo.

And it's no go the hullabaloo and all the lovey-dovey,
The nylon gloves, the dads in suits and the bridesmaids'
giggling covey.
And it's no go something borrowed teamed with new
and old and blue
For many couplings come apart before their first night's
through.

And bliss will not be guaranteed by horseshoe-shaped
confetti.
Aunt Mabel thought she'd found a prince but woke to
find a yeti.

(Continuing overleaf)

While the Bishop's wife woke up next day with love bites on her bum
And a firm resolve to sleep alone from then till kingdom come.

So it's no go bloody Cupid letting fly with showers of arrows
For those they hit may quickly find how soon love's prospect narrows.
And it's no go expecting him to find your perfect match
When his bow's more like a scatter-gun and his aim's not up to scratch.

With Robert Herrick and his Julia

(after his '*Upon Julia's Clothes*' – and with
apologies to them both)

Whenas in joy my Julia bounces
It vibrates all the pounds and ounces
Of both our spare tyres' sagging flounces.

Those tyres, the envy of Pirelli,
Protect like shock-absorbent jelly
Each time my Julia gives it welly.

But, though I try to play the foil,
For me love's still a risky toil
Till Julia's gone off the boil.

Whenas in time my Julia grows
less lustrous than a dew-pearled rose
I'll be the only one who knows.

For, while her unguents, paint and paste
applied with artistry and taste
may long conceal old age's haste

I'll do what timeless love entails
by doctoring her bathroom scales
to lie each day till my life fails.

John Donne as
Flea Circus Ringmaster

(ref: John Donne's '*The Flea*')

I've had a lover's bone to pick with thee
since thou wert penetrated by my flea.
For though our bloods be joined thou canst not see
thy way to share thy maidenhood with me.
But, as Ringmaster to troupes of fleas
well trained by me to bite and suck and tease
while mingling blood with any who agrees
to learn the arts of love by such degrees,
I soon could show thee, if thou would but see,
how much less coy flea-bitten maids can be.
And thus I'd hope one day thou might agree
that I could be a Ringmaster to thee
and hear thee change thy mind right eagerly
to conjoin more than bloods in ecstasy.

She Replies to Marlowe's Passionate Shepherd

(to "*Come live with me and be my love*")

I'll live with you and be your wife
And share your offered bed of roses
Although what horticulture shows is
Roses never last for life.

And on the verdant riverbanks
I'll prime your passion and I'll slake it
And sigh and moan, and mostly fake it,
And learn to never ask for thanks.

And I will risk Love's mocking laughter
At your dreams of life in clover
Until Love's furnace freezes over
Next year or the one thereafter.

Then, lest push should come to shove,
I'll stay with you and be your love,
If for no good reason other
Than to get away from Mother.

His 'Coy Mistress' Replies to Andrew Marvell

(saying that it is he, not she, who is
taking things too slowly)

A hundred years per eye and two per breast
And thirty thousand years for all the rest
Is using foreplay just for foreplay's sake
And for much longer than it ought to take.
Deft patience oft becomes a swain, 'tis said:
But if you go so slow we'll both be dead
Before you get to plant your flag and own
That part of me which you've not yet been shown
And boldly go where man has never been
To see those sights I'm eager should be seen.
'Tis you, my love, not I who is too coy
To plough the pasture which will yield us joy.
Time's winged chariot hurries ever near.
God grant it does not come 'ere you, my dear.
    This furrow waits the husbandry you'll show it.
    While you still may, come, aim your seed and sow it.

Leigh Hunt's '*Jenny*' Changes Her Mind

Jenny kissed me.
Sex, I deemed, would be consensual
Though written contracts seemed essential.
Their facts were writ in white and black.
She'd kissed me first, I'd kissed her back,
Consenting adults, willing lovers
There beneath her duvet covers;
As watertight as contracts get,

Unassailable. And yet
The Prosecution argued strongly
That I had treated Jenny wrongly
And must accept how she *now* saw
What happened forty years before
Was all that mattered under Law.
Now here in Belmarsh I regret
Jenny kissed me when we met.

Going to Bed with a Cheese and Pickle Sandwich

(a fantasy on a recommendation by poet, Mandy Coe)

I was lonely and depressed in Aston Purvis
staying in a very smart hotel
when I thought I'd test the talents of Room Service –
not a thing I often risk; but what the hell!
So, mindful of Ms. Coe, I thought the proper way to go
was to order up a cheese and pickle sandwich.

What arrived looked quite incredible, superlatively edible;
not the normal fare, a limp, white-sliced-loaf square
skimmed with Branston smeared on half a Kraft Cheese
Slice;
but made from finest Roquefort smelling rank as my old
sock drawer.
A sandwich worth its 3-star call-girl price.

Taking heed from Mandy Coe I felt I ought to let it know
I was not requiring poems, flowers or sex.
They all say that, *you know,* said its artisan sour-dough
as it curled its lip at what it feared I'd planned.
*Just remember, if you please, I'm made with very classy
cheese.*
I am not a one-night-quickie-cheeseboard-stand.

Don't think to be so silly as to wade in willy-nilly.
To reach my full potential I shall need you to be gentle.
Some foreplay is essential, plus a mood that's
reverential.
And also please remember that I'm not a one to stand
for a man who is too cock-sure with my Roquefort in his
hand . . .

Then I spent the next few days at a boarding-house in
Hayes
where they offered just three brands of English cheese,
disappointing in most ways and deserving little praise.
But by far the best of these in terms of eagerness to
please
were the foil-wrapped triangles of Dairylea
who begged me, *Don't be nervous. Lift the phone and*
call Room Service.

Then de-foil us and defile us, excite us and delight us.
Don't be gentle. Please go mental. Foreplay's wholly
inessential.
We will meet your every need. And, once you're
Dairylea'd,
with your taste buds subtly goaded and your senses
overloaded
you'll love your sandwich even more than Mandy Coe
did.

ENVIRONMENTAL CONCERNS

The Springtime of My Discontent

(after '*The Bloody Orkneys*' by Capt. Hamish Blair)

Bloody Springtime brings more rain,
Bloody lawn's all moss again.
Bloody wife wants garden dug,
Bloody job for bloody mug.
Bloody grass begins to grow,
Bloody mower will not mow.
Bloody next door's cat uproots
Bloody swathes of bloody shoots.

Bloody catalogues all lied,
Bloody plants all bloody died.
Bloody frame of greenhouse rotted,
Bloody knotweed bloody knotted.
Bloody frogs choke pond with spawn,
Bloody moles make Alps of lawn.
Chez Nous is a bloody mess.
Next door's like the RHS.

Maud Rejects Tennyson's Invitation

(to "*come into the garden*")

On the last of our joint horticultural trips
I contracted, I'm sorry to tell,
both black spot and mildew plus rose-mite and thrips
and you laddered my stockings as well.

So its all your own fault that I'll not be your guest
and that Nature's once bounteous charm
I can now only view with reluctance, at best,
and you with a sense of alarm.

For my mildew smells rank and my rose-mite now
stings
and I finally see what is true –
that my garden is full of some unwelcome things,
the least welcome of which being you.

So your now garden-phobic systemic-sprayed Maud
says that though you may temptingly coo
that the sweet "woodbine's spices are wafted abroad"
she wishes that you were there too.

The Wind Farm of Shalott

Last week Sir Lancelot came by
And clothed the wold and met the sky
With whirling monoliths on high
From here to Camelot.

Now all day long within my room
I'll hear their constant swish and boom
Until the very Crack of Doom
Supplying Camelot,

Where every cup of tea they make
And every bath and shower they take
Reminds me just how much I hate
The folk in Camelot.

And now he's here again, inspecting
Still more acres for erecting
Yet more turbines for injecting
Power to Camelot.

I can see him in my mirror.
On your way, sir. Tirra-lirra!
Prithee don't delay thee, sirrah.
Sod off back to Camelot!

Shalott Revisited

The Lady of Shalott
despised the folk of Camelot
who'd sent the lecher Lancelot
to try to wheedle and beguile her
into letting them defile her
views of barley and of rye
by building wind-farms close nearby
to power the lights of Camelot.

She left her web, she left her loom,
she fired a shotgun from her room.
And, though she missed Sir Lancelot,
two years in jail was what she got,
during which, we hear it told,
they redeveloped all her wold.
Now turbines sixty metres high
on either side the river lie.

The Curse of Wordsworth

I wandered with the package tour
which searched for Wordsworth's daffodils
when all at once I thought I saw
some grass, still living, on the hills.
Just six determined green young blades,
The only ones for two decades.

Big feet around them tramped and trod
in heavy hobnailed hiking boots;
each thoughtless, clumsy tourist clod
a threat to these last tender shoots –
beside the lake, beneath the trees,
the last things dancing in the breeze.

And now with every coach I pass
among the poet's lakeside hills
I worry for those blades of grass
and curse his bloody daffodils,
and wish that he had stayed in bed
and kept his landscapes in his head.

Wordsworth's Ghost Revisits Westminster Bridge

Earth had not anything to show more fair
when first I paused and wrote, a passer-by
who saw in London naught but majesty.
Yet London now doth like a felon wear
a prison house's stench from which each bare-
faced, money-grabbing, wild, lick-penny lie
doth rise, a Devil's incense, to the sky
and hangs like poison in the godless air.
Never did sun more hesitantly steep
above a banker's paunch or six-day bill
nor saw I Mammon gorging quite so deep.
The river cringeth past his fetid swill
where greed and counting houses never sleep,
the city's heart now but one mighty till.

Don't Let's Be Beastly
to The Poor Chinese

(after Noel Coward's '*Don't Let's Be Beastly
To The Germans*')

Don't let's be beastly to the poor Chinese
Whose lack of lab. security
May have started the dread disease
Which blighted our clean air's purity
And brought the World to its knees. . .

Nor remind them that, while eating bats
May be culturally totemic,
The facts suggest it's something that's
Helped to spread pandemic . . .

Nor rant at them and make a fuss.
There are more of them than there are of us
And they might throw us under their Chinese bus
Where we'd end up far more indisposed
Than even Sage had ever proposed . .

So, as Anglo/Sino relations face difficult times like
these,
Please don't let's be beastly to the poor Chinese.

Noel Coward on Council Flats

(after his '*The Stately Homes of England*')

The Council Flats of England were principally meant
to give the lower classes somewhere cheap to rent.
Though without a Moat and Banquet Hall
God only knows how they live at all
in such a tiny space.
But it keeps them in their place.

But soon the wicked Tax Man will force the rich to sell
all our family silver and our Stately Homes as well.
And after that we'll all reside
in whatever the Council can provide
as we drain the bitter cup
of levelling down, not up.

So, though their stairwells smell of fart
and are covered in quite revolting Art,
we'll stand by the Council Flats of England.

BARD ON THE RUN

On His First-Ever Folio

(by Shakespeare, Shakspere, Shaxper, et al.)

My teacher daily doth to me complain
of all the different ways I spell my name.
He says that if I cannot learn to spell
I've little chance of ever writing well.

One day I hope to show the witless clod
it doth not matter that my spelling's odd.
For greater things dictate, did he but know it,
if one's to be, or not to be, a famous poet.

The Bard Versus an Ikea Flat-pack

I must to the construction of this chair
Admit impediments. Ikea's goods
Are foolproof if the proper parts be there.
The bolts, the screws, instructions and the wood
Should be sufficient for correct construction;
But lacking the instructions, sad to tell,
I have been forced to make my own deductions
And these, 'tis plain to see, have not gone well.
Some madman, it appears, has been to town
For these be arms, I trow, where legs should be
And the upholstered seat is upside down.
My wife blames this, Ikea's fault, on me.
Had I but had instructions to peruse
I might now have a chair that I could use
And not this misbegotten alien species
Which, when I sit upon it, falls to pieces.

The Bard Rewires a Plug for his Dark Lady

The wiring of new-fangled plugs is changed
To colours of a wholly different hue,
Old reds and blacks and greens now re-arranged
As stripy yellow/green with brown and blue.
My own Dark Lady bids me now rewire
Her old device on which she sets great store
To help her light the flame of love's slow fire
That she may quicker play the wanton whore.
Yet, one new unfamiliar colour wired
In error in another colour's place
Could render this night's loving truly dire
And blast the smile from off my lady's face
Should we ignite, in foreplay's hurly-burly,
Her secret silken hairs both short and curly.
And if it could do that to such as she
God knows just what it might ignite of me.

Much Ado About Humpty Dumpty

A vaunting egg perched high upon a wall
Proclaimed himself the handsomest of fellows.
His shell he judged the brownest of them all,
His double yolk the yellowest of yellows.
Then, lo! The prating coxcomb tumbled down
And in the wretched dust was equal made
With those whose hapless shells were less dark brown
And much cracked from the strain of being laid.
No use to him the King's men and their horses
Who chanced upon his body spread around
But lacked a skilled physician's deft resources
To reassemble all the bits they found.
   An egg, they said, fit but for one Last Post
   From eager soldiers made of buttered toast.

Almost All the World's a Stage

Bard –
   Most generous and noble Patron, hark!
   Methinks I have a bold new-fangled plan
   To show life in a lowly London square,
   And plumb each depth of direst human tedium
   For half a dreary hour four nights each week
   To run, relentless, till the crack of doom.
   My Cast is one to catch the common shilling.
   No kings nor queens nor princes will there be,
   No fancy folk of note from foreign lands;
   But just a motley crowd of crude plebeians
   All fired by lust and greed and lack of brain
   Who speak in curses, grunts and grating vowels
   With ne'er a consonant to put between,
   Who lead their wretched lives of sordid drama
   As bare of lustre as a kitchen sink,
   With naught for entertainment but an inn
   Ill-run by screeching harridans from Hell,
   One dwarfish but with ample teats which fed
   Two slap-head sons of thuggish attitude
   Both much enamoured with an orange wench
   Whose eyes and breasts both overact on cue
   At each of daily life's vicissitudes;
   Plus varied surly, rude mechanicals
   Involved in aspects of the carriage trade

And one deluded soul who finds how small
The need in Walford is for tired fresh vegetables.

Discerning Patron –

Enough, I beg! I have one basic gripe.
What fool would pay to watch such dreary tripe?
You, with your knowledge, surely cannot hope
I'd finance drama drear as scentless soap.
Our public at The Globe would soon be bored.
Make all the world your stage – except for Walford!

Enter Soothsayer

Soothsayer –

Keep, I suggest these thoughts which you have aired
Until the birth of one John Logie Baird;
For that which now brings scorn and vile derision
May be one day much prized on television
Which may, too, stage your last week's master-stroke –
A Coronation tale of northern folk.

The Dark Lady's Concern
About Sonnet 130

*('my mistress' eyes are nothing like the sun;
. . . if snow be white, why then, her breasts be dun')*

E'er since you told the world my breasts be dun
Your wife has known by whom they've been undone.
And she may wonder how far you've progressed
With other parts of me which you've undressed
As from my eager dark moist lips you sup
To drain the nightly joys of love's sweet cup,
And in my wiry muff to parse love's grammar
Which drives thy deep-dipped quill's insistent clamour.
Yea, dark I be in all my privvy parts
Yet deeper-dark am I in love's dark arts.
Now of my skills should Anne be sore afeared
And you to her now somewhat less endeared.
　　Mayhap you should withdraw this latest sonnet,
　　Else may your marriage end in grief upon it.

The Dark Lady
Switches Allegiance

When I consider how I wrote each play
You ever claimed as yours, you worthless blighter,
How sharper than a serpent's tooth I say
It is to love a thankless, third-rate writer.
Know this, my self-styled Bard, you sore abuse
The one you know is author of your work,
The one whose name you will not let me use.
You cheating, ingrate, balding, little berk!
No more I'll grasp your withered, blunted quill
And shape love's torrid lines upon your bed,
Nor strive to grind out other lines that will
Be claimed to be *your* copyright instead.

    By this Dark Lady you are now forsaken.
    I'm off! – to write for cash and Francis Bacon.

Wishful Thinking

I scratch my Bardic pate and roundly curse
And yearn to write in deathless lines that don't
Emerge as sonnets or as dull blank verse.
But Gloriana's taste, I fear, now won't
Accept the slightest hint of metric change.
And this demand of hers means that I can't
O'er step one jot the limits of her range.
Thus, for preferment's fickle sake, I shan't.
Yet in my heart still beats the rebel urge
To flee this Court and strut a different stage,
Where matched pentameters do not converge
In perfect symmetry on every page.
    Of blank verse and of sonnets I am sick.
    Sweet Christ, that I might write one limerick!

The Play's the Thing

Julius Caesar

Politicians all huggery-muggery
And hell-bent on violent skulduggery
Knife one of their own
And are pretty soon shown
The cost of political thuggery.

The Taming of the Shrew

Feminists all, be ashamed.
Subjugation by man can be blamed
For this comic farrago
In which a virago
Submits to be married and tamed.

The Winter's Tale

In iambics for page after page
There's plotting, confusion and rage.
But it's fair to reveal
This play's major appeal
Is the bear that's the last off the stage.

Small Ads. from Shakespeare

Wanted –

Danish gravedigger raking over old ground
Seeks rest of body for the head he's found.

   Successful play-write, though no rich man he,
   Seeks generous sponsor to set up RSC.

Humble spear carrier in need of greater recognition,
And hoping to develop his career, needs bigger spear.

   A bear to close Act 3 Scene 4 with frantic chase.
   Must be slow and toothless – just in case!

For Sale –

Whole kingdom going cheap perforce
To knight with serviceable horse.

   Egyptian asp, now safe in basket after much travail.
   Late owner now in casket. Hence Executors' Sale.

Nice arras with small hole and vestiges of gore.
Apply: Mrs Polonius, Elsinore.

   Three Scottish vivisectionists will sell
   Old cauldron cheaply due to lingering smell.

Lonely Hearts –

Tragic walled-in lover hopes his soul may
Find another to go the hole way.

   Successful Emperor, without a doubt the greatest,
   Seeks Senators for lasting friendship –
   by the Ides of March at latest.

Shakespeare. The View
from St. Custard's

If A.A. Milne had been The Bard
English exams would be less hard.

(from my own First Folio)

Signed, Nigel Molesworth
            (aka Mulewart, Molewerf, Malewhiff, etc, etc.)

FESTIVE CHEER

the nativity in a nutshell

(after e. e. cummings's '*may i feel said he*')

room to stay said she
no way said he
no bed said she
a shed said he

nothing more said she
some straw said he
livestock said she
en bloc said he

i'm in pod said she
via god said she
strewth said he
it's the truth said she

here's the place said he
watch this space said she
sleep tight said he
not tonight said she

To Santa . . . from Dorothy Parker

*(who wanted more than yet another
"perfect bloody rose.")*

That limousine! You've still not brought mine yet.
This broad now reckons it's high time to get
a Cadillac, for preference, or an Oldsmobile,
a Studebaker, Buick or a Coupe de Ville –
not one more perfect bloody rose.
Maybe a Packard, Chrysler or a Cord
or at the very least a top-range Ford
(though not an Edsel, Santa, I implore).
This dame has pressing need to ask for more
than one more perfect bloody rose,
so folk at The Algonquin can applaud
each day when she's post-prandially poured
into a car that reeks, Oy vey, of money's stench.

Dear Santa, super-uber Merry Christmas Mensch,
please not another perfect bloody rose!

Maya Angelou's Turkey

(after her '*And Still I Rise*')

You may strip me of my breast meat,
of my drumsticks, wings and thighs.
You may think that I am finished;
but on Boxing Day I'll rise.

When you've served me cold with pickle
and the weariest of sighs
you'll be certain I am done with;
but like Lazarus I'll rise.

You will think that you have sampled
all the woes that Yule can bring.
But as curry, soup and rissoles
I might well go on till Spring.

I may bore you and revolt you,
I might even make you ill.
But I'll last a whole lot longer
Than your Christmas Spirit will.

These Be The Songs

(after Philip Larkin's '*This Be The Verse*')

They fuck you up, child carol singers.
Each Christmas I am sure they mean to.
Those pint-sized Yuletide goodwill bringers
should all be summarily seen to.

So *we* should fuck *them* up instead
by being ruthlessly hard-hearted
and stop them messing with our heads
before each group of them gets started.

Man hands tone deafness to his kids
then sends them round to sing us carols.
So, keep a shotgun by your door
and give the little dears both barrels.

Leonard Cohen's
Christmas Hallelujah

Once more you'll wake and greet the way
a child is born on Christmas Day
with loving presents given by or to yah.
And kids will puke and fight and shout
and Ma will over-boil each sprout
to celebrate the baby. *Hallelujah!*

In just a few weeks, give or take,
they'll nail him to a wooden stake.
But you don't care so much for dying, do yah?
For thorns and nails are not the same,
and chocolate eggs are pretty lame
compared to stars and shepherds. *Hallelujah!*

Perhaps there's still a God above.
Though now the world is short of love
and anger and despair may soon eat through yah
while common-sense is put on hold
and all that glitters is fools' gold
it's hard to raise a Christmas *Hallelujah!*

Tennyson's Hopes
for the New Year

Ring out, wild bells, on midnight's stroke
To dock Woke's tail which wags our dog
And clouds old truths in specious fog.
Ring out to toll the knell for Woke.

Ring out, wild bells, and drown the sound
Of BBC's PC agendas
And raucous rants from gender blenders.
Let calm regain the centre ground.

Ring out, wild bells, to shame Woke's devil
And those who earn their Woke-smeared crust
From Academe and National Trust
And public life at every level.

Ring in a new resolve in Britain
To stem the rampant epidemic
Of Woke's insidious polemic.
Ring in the year Woke's Hydra's stricken.

Eeyore at Christmas

Harrumph! to the Christmas Spirit,
and Humbug! to Seasonal Cheer
which lasts for a week in December
and dies with the bells of New Year.

Then pine needles clog up the Hoover
and problems pile up by the yard.
Good Wishes are too often transient things,
whatever it says on the card.

Milton Keynes UK
Ingram Content Group UK Ltd.
UKHW010613131023
430517UK00005B/84